Audit of the Financial Stability Oversight Council's Designation of Financial Market Utilities

Report to the Financial Stability Oversight Council and the Congress

PREPARED BY
THE COUNCIL OF INSPECTORS GENERAL
ON FINANCIAL OVERSIGHT

JULY 2013

Table of Contents

Transmittal Letter 1

Executive Summary 2

Results of CIGFO Working Group Review 5

    FSOC's Process for Designating FMUs 7

    FSOC's Process For Monitoring FMUs 12

    Conclusion and Recommendations 12

APPENDICES

    APPENDIX I: Objective, Scope and Methodology 15

    APPENDIX II: Timeline of Significant FMU Designation Events 16

    APPENDIX III: Description of Designated FMUs 17

    APPENDIX IV: FSOC Response 20

    APPENDIX V: CIGFO Working Group 22

Abbreviations and Acronyms

ANPR	Advanced notice of proposed rulemaking
CFTC	Commodity Futures Trading Commission
CHIPS	Clearing House Interbank Payments System
CIGFO	Council of Inspectors General on Financial Oversight
CME	Chicago Mercantile Exchange, Inc.
Dodd-Frank Act	Dodd-Frank Wall Street Reform and Consumer Protection Act
DTC	The Depository Trust Company
FICC	Fixed Income Clearing Corporation
FMU	Financial market utility
FRB	Board of Governors of the Federal Reserve System
FSOC or Council	Financial Stability Oversight Council
ICE Clear Credit	ICE Clear Credit LLC
NPR	Notice of proposed rulemaking
NSCC	National Securities Clearing Corporation
OFR	Office of Financial Research
PCS	Payment, clearing, and settlement
SEC	U.S. Securities and Exchange Commission
Title I	Dodd-Frank Wall Street Reform and Consumer Protection Act, Title I—Financial Stability
Title VIII	Dodd-Frank Wall Street Reform and Consumer Protection Act, Title VIII—Payment, Clearing, and Settlement Supervision
Treasury	The Department of the Treasury

DEPARTMENT OF THE TREASURY
WASHINGTON, D.C. 20220

July 12, 2013

The Honorable Jacob J. Lew
Chair, Financial Stability Oversight Council
Washington, D.C. 20220

Dear Mr. Chairman:

I am pleased to present you with the Council of Inspectors General on Financial Oversight (CIGFO) report titled, Audit of the Financial Stability Oversight Council's Designation of Financial Market Utilities.

As the designation of financial market utilities (FMUs) is one of the key authorities given to FSOC by the Dodd-Frank Wall Street Reform and Consumer Protection Act, I proposed convening a working group to assess the rules, procedures, and practices established by FSOC and its members to determine which FMUs should be designated as systemically important. The proposal was approved, and a CIGFO Working Group completed a review.

This CIGFO report recommends that FSOC (1) establish a formal structure for the FMU Committee; (2) determine a course of action with regard to foreign-based FMUs consistent with the authorities of Title VIII; (3) continue deliberations on the process and rules regarding possible future designation of payment, clearing and settlement activities conducted by financial institutions; (4) define the nature, frequency, and communication of updates on designated FMUs from the FMU regulators; and (5) establish a timeline for periodic reviews of non-designated FMUs that may be systemically important.

I would like to take this opportunity to thank the support of the FSOC members, especially those Treasury officials who assisted with this effort.

CIGFO looks forward to working with you on this and other issues. In accordance with the Dodd-Frank Act, CIGFO is also providing this report to Congress.

Sincerely,

Eric M. Thorson
Chair
Council of Inspectors General on Financial Oversight

Enclosure

Executive Summary

Why and How We Conducted the Review

The Dodd-Frank Wall Street Reform and Consumer Protection Act (Dodd-Frank Act) created a comprehensive regulatory and resolution framework designed to reduce the severe economic consequences of economic instability. The Financial Stability Oversight Council (FSOC or the Council), established by the Dodd-Frank Act, is charged with identifying risks to the nation's financial stability, promoting market discipline, and responding to emerging threats to the stability of the nation's financial system. Title VIII of the Dodd-Frank Act–Payment, Clearing, and Settlement Supervision (Title VIII), authorizes FSOC to designate financial market utilities (FMUs) as "systemically important" if FSOC determines that the failure or a disruption to the functioning of the FMU could create or increase the risk of significant liquidity or credit problems spreading among financial institutions or markets and thereby threaten the stability of the U.S. financial system. FSOC-designated FMUs are then subject to enhanced risk management requirements and enhanced supervision under Title VIII. On July 18, 2012, FSOC voted unanimously to designate eight FMUs as systemically important.

> **Financial market utilities** are systems that provide the essential infrastructure for transferring, clearing, and settling payments, securities, and other financial transactions among financial institutions or between financial institutions and the system.

The Dodd-Frank Act also established the Council of Inspectors General on Financial Oversight (CIGFO). CIGFO's statutory functions include oversight of FSOC. In this regard, the law authorizes CIGFO to convene a working group, by a majority vote, for the purpose of evaluating the effectiveness and internal operations of FSOC. In January 2013, Eric Thorson, CIGFO Chair and Department of the Treasury (Treasury) Inspector General, proposed convening a working group to assess the application of the rules, procedures, and practices established by FSOC and its members to determine which FMUs should be designated as systemically important and therefore subject to the requirements of Title VIII. CIGFO unanimously approved the proposal and formed a Working Group.

To accomplish its objective, the CIGFO Working Group reviewed the processes and procedures FSOC used to designate the eight FMUs as systemically important. As part of that review, the Working Group reviewed (1) how FSOC established the universe of FMUs for consideration and (2) FSOC processes going forward to review FMU activity, to designate additional FMUs and, when appropriate, to rescind an FMU designation.

What We Learned

Title VIII authorizes certain activities for FSOC to perform during the FMU designation process. These activities include, among others, prescribing rules to administer FSOC's authority to designate FMUs as systemically important, requesting information from FMUs, consulting with regulatory agencies, and providing FMUs with notice of final determination of designation. We determined that FSOC carried out the designation activities as established in Title VIII with respect to the designation of the eight FMUs as systemically important.

To assist in carrying out the designation activities, FSOC created the Designations of Financial Market Utilities and Payment, Clearing, and Settlement Activities Committee (FMU Committee). In obtaining information during the designation process, the FMU Committee relied on the FSOC member agencies that regulate FMUs, namely the Commodity Futures Trading Commission (CFTC), the Board of Governors of the Federal Reserve System (FRB), and the U.S. Securities and Exchange Commission (SEC).[1] Although the FMU Committee did not have final decision-making authority, preliminary recommendations during the FMU designation process were made at the FMU Committee level and then moved through the Deputies Committee[2] to FSOC for a final vote. We found that the FMU Committee carried out its activities in the designation process as intended by FSOC. However, we noted that the FMU Committee did not have a designated chairperson and did not keep a record of its meetings.

We also learned that during the FMU designation process, FSOC decided not to consider for designation at this time, foreign-based FMUs; retail FMUs;[3] or payment, clearing, and settlement (PCS) activities conducted by financial institutions. However, we were told that deliberations continue within FSOC regarding (1) foreign-based FMUs and (2) the designations of PCS activities. We were also told that the designation of retail FMUs is not part of the Council's current work and that no estimate of when or if retail FMUs will be designated has been established.[4]

While the Council relies on the respective regulators of the designated FMUs to monitor their activities and report updates to the Council, there is no agreement or process established in writing by FSOC that defines the nature, frequency, and communication of such updates. Additionally, since the designation of eight FMUs in July 2012, FSOC has not conducted additional reviews of FMUs that may be systemically important, nor has it established a schedule for doing so.

Recommendations

Because of the critical role the FMU Committee will likely play in the future, we are recommending that FSOC establish a formal structure for the FMU Committee, including designating a chairperson and keeping a record of committee meetings to document, among other things, its deliberations and key recommendations.

Regarding foreign-based FMUs, we are recommending that FSOC determine a course of action consistent with its authorities, as foreign-based FMUs may be systemically important to the stability of the U.S.

---

[1] According to FSOC staff, this reliance was based on two important factors: (1) these regulatory agencies were the ones with subject matter expertise on FMUs, and (2) in part, to reduce the burden on companies under consideration. To the extent that regulatory agencies already had information relevant to the designation process, the Council relied on the agencies to provide this data rather than request that each company re-submit information, thus reducing the burden on the companies.

[2] The Deputies Committee coordinates and oversees the work of the interagency staff committees and is made up of a senior official from each FSOC member agency.

[3] Retail FMUs, such as MasterCard and Visa, manage or operate systems for mostly consumer payments of relatively low value and urgency.

[4] In this regard, the final rule on designating FMUs as systemically important articulates the Council's rationale, namely that these retail payments systems are generally low-value systems for which there appear to be readily available and timely alternative payment mechanisms.

financial system. Because Title VIII authorizes FSOC to designate PCS activities conducted by financial institutions as systemically important, the Council should also continue its deliberations on the possible future designation of PCS activities.

We are recommending that FSOC define the nature, frequency, and communication of updates on designated FMUs from the respective regulators of the FMUs. We are also recommending that FSOC establish a timeline for periodic reviews of non-designated FMUs that may be systemically important.

FSOC Response

In a written response, FSOC stated that with respect to the recommendation to establish a formal structure for the FMU Committee, the Council is examining ways to further enhance the governance of the Council's staff committees. In regard to the recommendations on foreign-based FMUs and PCS activities, the FMU Committee is expected to continue its discussions on these matters at its upcoming meetings and will communicate any developments to the Deputies Committee and the Council as appropriate. Specific procedures and rules for the future designation of PCS activities are not being considered by the FMU Committee at this time, but may be developed in the future. The FMU Committee will be asked to continue the work it has begun by proposing specific procedures to address the recommendations on updates on designated FMUs from the FMU regulators and establishing a timeline for periodic reviews of non-designated FMUs. FSOC's response is provided as Appendix IV.

CIGFO Working Group Comments

As a whole, we consider FSOC's commitments and planned actions responsive to our recommendations. We recognize that certain commitments and planned actions are matters of on-going work of the FMU Committee and the Council. For other actions, FSOC should establish estimated completion dates for implementation.

Results of CIGFO Working Group Review

Introduction

Title VIII authorizes FSOC to designate FMUs as systemically important if FSOC determines that the failure of or a disruption to the functioning of the FMU could create or increase the risk of significant liquidity or credit problems spreading among financial institutions or markets and thereby threaten the stability of the U.S. financial system. This report presents the results of the CIGFO Working Group's audit of FSOC's implementation of Title VIII. This is the second report that a CIGFO Working Group has issued to the Council and the Congress as part of CIGFO's responsibility to oversee FSOC under the Dodd-Frank Act. CIGFO issued its first report in June 2012. That report discussed the results of CIGFO's examination of the controls and protocols that FSOC and its federal agency members employ to safeguard from unauthorized disclosure, non-public information collected by, and exchanged with, FSOC federal agency members.[5]

Background

FSOC was established to create joint accountability for identifying and mitigating potential threats to the stability of the nation's financial system. By creating FSOC, Congress recognized that financial stability would require the collective engagement of the entire financial regulatory community.

As shown in the table on the next page, FSOC consists of 10 voting members and 5 nonvoting members and brings together the expertise of federal financial regulators, state regulators, and an insurance expert appointed by the President with Senate confirmation.

Table 1: FSOC Membership	
Federal and Independent Members	**State Members**
• Secretary of the Department of the Treasury, Chairperson (v) • Chairman of the Board of Governors of the Federal Reserve System (v) • Comptroller of the Currency (v) • Director of the Consumer Financial Protection Bureau (v) • Chairman of the Securities and Exchange Commission (v) • Chairperson of the Federal Deposit Insurance Corporation (v) • Chairperson of the Commodity Futures Trading Commission (v) • Director of the Federal Housing Finance Agency (v) • Chairman of the National Credit Union Administration Board (v) • Director of the Office of Financial Research • Director of the Federal Insurance Office • Independent member with insurance expertise (v) (v) Indicates Voting Member	• State Insurance Commissioner • State Banking Supervisor • State Securities Commissioner

---

5   CIGFO, Audit of the Financial Stability Oversight Council's Controls over Non-public Information, (June 22, 2012).

The purposes of FSOC are to:

- identify risks to the financial stability of the U S. that could arise from the material financial distress or failure, or ongoing activities, of large, interconnected bank holding companies or nonbank financial companies, or that could arise outside the financial services marketplace;

- promote market discipline, by eliminating expectations on the part of shareholders, creditors, and counterparties of such companies that the U.S. Government will shield them from losses in the event of failure; and

- respond to emerging threats to the stability of the U S. financial system.

Within Treasury, a dedicated policy office, led by a Deputy Assistant Secretary, functions as the FSOC Secretariat and serves as a mechanism to bring issues to the Council through a coordinated process. Voting members of FSOC provide a federal regulatory perspective and an independent insurance expert's view. The nonvoting members offer different insights as state-level representatives from bank, securities, and insurance regulators or as the directors of offices within Treasury – the Office of Financial Research (OFR) and the Federal Insurance Office.

To carry out its mission, FSOC uses a committee structure.[6] Individual committees handle key responsibilities and are staffed by personnel from FSOC members. For example, the FMU Committee supports FSOC in identifying, recommending, and reviewing designations of FMUs and PCS activities as systemically important. Recommendations and activities of the FMU Committee are subject to review by the Deputies Committee and ultimate decision-making authority is retained by the Council itself.

Congress made the following findings in Title VIII:

- The proper functioning of the financial markets is dependent upon safe and efficient arrangements for the clearing and settlement of payment, securities, and other financial transactions.

- FMUs that conduct or support multilateral PCS activities may reduce risks for their participants and the broader financial system, but such utilities may also concentrate and create new risks and thus must be well designed and operated in a safe and sound manner.

- PCS activities conducted by financial institutions also present important risks to the participating financial institutions and to the financial system.

- Enhancements to the regulation and supervision of systemically important FMUs and the conduct of systemically important PCS activities by financial institutions are necessary to provide consistency, promote robust risk management and safety and soundness, reduce systemic risks, and support the stability of the broader financial system.

---

6   FSOC's committee structure includes the Deputies Committee and the Systemic Risk Committee. The Systemic Risk Committee has two sub-committees – the Institutions Sub-committee and the Markets Sub-committee. There are also five Standing Functional Committees – the Designations of Nonbank Financial Companies Committee; the FMU Committee; the Heightened Prudential Standards Committee; the Orderly Liquidation Authority, Resolution Plans Committee; and the Data Committee.

In addition, Congress stated that the purpose of Title VIII is to mitigate systemic risk in the financial system and promote financial stability by:

- authorizing FRB to promote uniform standards for the (1) management of risks by systemically important FMUs and (2) conduct of systemically important payment, clearing, and settlement activities by financial institutions;

- providing FRB an enhanced role in the supervision of risk management standards for systemically important FMUs;

- strengthening the liquidity of systemically important FMUs; and

- providing FRB an enhanced role in the supervision of risk management standards for systemically important payment, clearing, and settlement activities by financial institutions.

Audit Approach

The objective of our audit was to assess the rules, procedures, and practices established by FSOC and its members to determine which FMUs should be designated as systemically important and therefore be subject to the enhanced risk management and supervision provisions of Title VIII. We conducted our audit fieldwork from February through April 2013 in accordance with generally accepted government auditing standards.

As members of the CIGFO Working Group, each participating Office of Inspector General collected information on its FSOC federal member(s) regarding FSOC's process for designating FMUs. We collected similar information from the FSOC Secretariat and FSOC non-federal members. The information was gathered using a CIGFO Working Group-developed questionnaire and document request based on the designation process activities outlined in Title VIII.

The Working Group participants presented the results of their respective questionnaires and document reviews to the applicable FSOC member and FSOC Secretariat, who were given the opportunity to provide additional comments. We consolidated and reviewed the results to determine and assess FSOC's process for designating FMUs and to identify potential opportunities to strengthen the process. We provided an exit briefing on the overall results of our work to FSOC representatives on May 31, 2013.

FSOC's Process for Designating FMUs

FSOC Followed Designation Process Activities Outlined in Title VIII

Title VIII gives FSOC the authority, on a non-delegable basis and by a vote of no fewer than two-thirds of members then serving, including an affirmative vote by the Chairperson of the Council (the Secretary of the Treasury), to designate those FMUs that FSOC determines are, or are likely to become, systemically important.

To help carry out its authority to designate FMUs as systemically important, FSOC established the FMU Committee, one of five standing functional committees. According to the FSOC Secretariat, the FMU Committee is a collaborative, staff-level group that supports the work of the Council, and operates on a consensus basis; its discussions and work products are deliberative in nature. The FSOC Secretariat stated the committee has no autonomous decision-making authority delegated to it by the Council. However, preliminary recommendations regarding the designation of FMUs were made at the FMU Committee level and then moved through the Deputies Committee to the Council, which made the final decisions. Examples of recommendations made by the FMU Committee included: (1) the wording of various versions of the advanced notice of proposed rulemaking (ANPR),[7] the notice of proposed rulemaking (NPR),[8] the final rule[9] as well as the subcategories of the considerations listed in the final rule; and (2) the identification and recommendation of the eight FMUs that the Council ultimately voted on for designation as systemically important.

The FMU Committee held its initial meeting in January 2011 and then generally met monthly from March to November 2011. The FMU Committee began meeting more frequently from January to May 2012 as FSOC's final determination on designating FMUs neared in July 2012. Since May 2012, the FMU Committee has met three times. Examples of discussion items during the these meetings included updates on designated FMUs, the process for considering additional FMUs for designation, and the framework for periodically reviewing designated FMUs.

We determined that FSOC carried out designation activities established in Title VIII. The activities are described below.

> Determining considerations - *Title VIII specified that FSOC take into consideration the following when determining whether an FMU is or is likely to become systemically important.*

- The aggregate monetary value of transactions processed by the FMU
- The aggregate exposure of the FMU to its counterparties[10]
- The relationship, interdependencies, or other interactions of the FMU with other FMUs or PCS activities
- The effect that the failure of or disruption to the FMU would have on critical markets, financial institutions, or the broader financial system
- Any other factors the Council deems appropriate

In its final rule, which is described below, FSOC incorporated these considerations but did not identify any other factors in accordance with the fifth consideration.

> Rulemaking - Title VIII authorizes FSOC to prescribe rules and issue orders to administer its authority for the designation process. FSOC published an ANPR on December 21, 2010, regarding the designation criteria, followed by the publication of a NPR on March 28, 2011. The ANPR invited public comment on the criteria and analytical framework that should be applied by the Council in designating FMUs under Title VIII. The NPR described: (1) the FMU designation processes and procedures established under the Dodd-Frank Act and (2) the criteria to be used by the Council for determining systemic importance of FMUs.

The Council published the final rule on July 27, 2011, which included a two-stage designation process described in the NPR. Stage One consists of a data-driven process to result in the FMU Committee identifying

---

7 75 Fed. Reg. 79,982

8 76 Fed. Reg. 17,047

9 76 Fed. Reg. 44,763

10 Counterparties include other participants in a financial transaction.

a preliminary set of FMUs for possible designation. During Stage One, the FMU Committee considers factors such as, but not limited to, the number of transactions processed, cleared, or settled by the FMU; the value of transactions processed, cleared, or settled by the FMU; credit exposures to counterparties; the role of an FMU in the market served; and the availability of substitutes. During Stage Two, the FMUs identified in Stage One undergo a more in-depth review, with a greater focus on qualitative factors, in addition to other institutional and market specific considerations.

> Requesting information – To assist in its assessment of whether an FMU is systemically important, Title VIII authorizes FSOC to request information, reports, or records directly from the FMU under consideration. In this regard, Title VIII requires FSOC to coordinate first with the FMU's appropriate regulatory agency to obtain this information. For the most part, during the designation process, FSOC relied on its agency members who were also the FMUs' regulators (CFTC, FRB, and SEC) to communicate with the FMUs for the purpose of obtaining information.

FSOC member agencies told us that the information they received for the purposes of evaluating each FMU under consideration for designation was adequate. During our review, we inquired whether OFR[11] had a role in the designation process for the eight FMUs. We were told that OFR did not play a role.

> Consultation with supervisory agencies – Title VIII requires FSOC to consult with the relevant regulatory agency and the FRB before making any determinations of designation or rescission. The FSOC Secretariat stated that the FMU Committee consulted with and relied on input from the FMU regulators, which included the FRB, to determine the population of FMUs to be considered for designation because the regulators had the expertise. During the designation process, methods used for consultation with the FMU regulators and among the FMU Committee members included email correspondence, in-person meetings, telephone conferences, and document and information sharing via SharePoint.

> Advance notice of proposed determination – Title VIII requires FSOC to provide FMUs with advance notice of the proposed determination of the Council, and offer the FMUs the opportunity to request a hearing within 30 days from the date of the advance notice.

In a memorandum dated December 19, 2011, the FMU Committee unanimously recommended to the Council, through the Deputies Committee, that eight FMUs be advanced from Stage One to Stage Two of the designation process. On December 21, 2011, the Council voted unanimously to approve the eight FMUs advancement to Stage Two. In letters dated January 4, 2012, FSOC provided written notices to the eight FMUs that the Council was considering them for a proposed determination, and invited the eight FMUs to submit information to FSOC for or against the proposed designations. According to the FSOC Secretariat, several FMUs responded by submitting information about their companies that further helped in the designation process, and one FMU requested a meeting with FSOC staff to discuss concerns regarding the competitive implications of being designated. The FSOC Secretariat stated the requested meeting was not considered to be a formal hearing in the context of Title VIII.

---

11 Created under Title I of the Dodd-Frank Act, the purpose of OFR is to support FSOC in fulfilling the purposes and duties of the Council, and to support member agencies, by (1) collecting data on behalf of the Council, and providing such data to the Council and member agencies; (2) standardizing the types and formats of data reported and collected; (3) performing applied research and essential long-term research; (4) developing tools for risk measurement and monitoring; (5) performing other related services; (6) making the results of the activities of the office available to financial regulatory agencies; and (7) assisting such member agencies in determining the types and formats of data authorized by the act to be collected by such member agencies.

On May 22, 2012, FSOC sent letters informing the eight FMUs that the Council proposed to designate each entity systemically important. The letters provided advance notice of proposed designation and informed each FMU of its right to request a hearing on or before June 21, 2012. None of the eight FMUs requested a hearing.

Final vote – As authorized by Title VIII, FSOC voted on July 18, 2012, to designate the eight FMUs as systemically important. The eight designated FMUs are the same eight FMUs that received the notice of the proposed designation in May 2012.

Notice of final determination - In letters dated July 18, 2012, FSOC notified the eight FMUs of the final determination of the Council, as required by Title VIII.[12] As authorized by the Dodd-Frank Act, CFTC, FRB, and SEC separately established through a rulemaking process, additional standards for designated FMUs under their supervisory authority. The eight designated FMUs and their regulators are listed in Table 2. We provide a description of the eight designated FMUs in Appendix III.

Table 2: Eight FMUs Designated as Systemically Important

Financial Market Utility	Regulator for purposes of Title VIII
The Clearing House Payments Company, L.L.C., on the basis of its role as operator of the Clearing House Interbank Payments System (CHIPS	FRB
CLS Bank International	FRB
Chicago Mercantile Exchange, Inc.	CFTC
The Depository Trust Company	SEC
Fixed Income Clearing Corporation	SEC
ICE Clear Credit LLC	CFTC
National Securities Clearing Corporation	SEC
The Options Clearing Corporation	SEC

We concluded that the FMU designation process followed by FSOC conformed to Title VIII. Our review, however, identified the following areas for improvement or continuing effort by FSOC related to the FMU Committee structure and deliberations on designating foreign-based FMUs and PCS activities.

---

12   FSOC also issued a press release the same day announcing the designations of the eight FMUs.

FSOC Should Establish a Formal FMU Committee Structure

While the FMU Committee supported FSOC in the designation process, it operated in a somewhat unstructured manner. It did not have a charter or a designated chairperson. The FMU Committee had meeting agendas, but it did not keep a record of its meetings to document whether the committee discussed the agenda items or to provide detail on the Committee's deliberations or recommendations. In a September 2012 report, the Government Accountability Office (GAO) noted a similar absence of detailed records on the part of FSOC and its committees, and how this made it difficult to assess FSOC's performance.[13]

The FSOC Secretariat stated that the FMU Committee wanted an open and collaborative process. The FSOC Secretariat also stated that at the FMU Committee's most recent meeting on March 20, 2013, there was some discussion of formalizing certain aspects of the FMU Committee structure. While FSOC's committees are not required by law to keep a record of its meetings,[14] we believe it is important to document: (1) recommendations made, (2) agreed upon actions to be taken, and (3) assignment of any tasks or responsibilities. Such a record would also provide the means for assessing committee performance over time and may be useful to new FMU committee members. Furthermore, keeping a record of meetings should not hinder the FMU Committee's desire for an open and collaborative process.

FSOC Should Determine a Course of Action with Regard to Foreign-based FMUs and Continue Deliberations on the Process and Rules Regarding Possible Future Designation of PCS Activities as Systemically Important

During Stage One of the FMU designation process, FSOC identified certain foreign-based FMUs as potential candidates for designation as systemically important. However, FSOC decided not to pursue possible designation at the time pending further deliberations. According to the FSOC Secretariat, this matter is still under review.

Also, in its final rule on designations of FMUs, FSOC acknowledged its Title VIII authority to designate PCS activities conducted by financial institutions as systemically important and stated that it expects to address these designations in a separate rulemaking. As of May 2013, FSOC had not published a proposed rule for the designation of PCS activities as systemically important. The FSOC Secretariat told us that the FMU Committee discussed this point at its two most recent meetings (in December 2012 and March 2013) and further discussions are expected on the matter.

In its work going forward, FSOC should determine a course of action with regard to foreign-based FMUs consistent with its authorities and continue deliberations on the processes and rules regarding possible future designations of PCS activities as systemically important.

---

[13] GAO, Financial Stability: New Council and Research Office Should Strengthen the Accountability and Transparency of Their Decisions (GAO-12-886; Sept. 2012). In the report, GAO stated that while FSOC released minutes from its meetings as required by its bylaws, it did not keep detailed records of deliberations or discussions that take place at these meetings or at the committee level. GAO also stated that while no specific level of detail was required for FSOC minutes, the limited documentation of discussions made it difficult to assess FSOC's performance.

[14] As the seminal statute on government committees, the Federal Advisory Committee Act (FACA) outlines several guidelines and requirements that must be followed such as the creation of a charter before any business is conducted, public notification of committee meetings in the Federal Register, and the keeping of minutes. However, the DoddFrank Act states that FACA does not apply to FSOC or to any special advisory, technical, or professional committee appointed by the Council, except that, if such a committee has one or more members who are not employees of or affiliated with the U.S. Government, the Council shall publish a list of names of the members of such committee.

With regard to retail FMUs, the final rule on the designation of FMUs as systemically important states "FSOC has decided against including in the final rule any categorical exclusion for FMUs operating retail payment or other systems, because there are not clear distinctions between various types of systems, and because such an exclusion would impair the Council's ability to respond appropriately to new information, changed circumstances, and future developments." In addition, the final rule states that the Council does not expect to focus on "FMUs that operate low-value systems for which there appear to be readily available and timely alternative payment mechanisms," including retail payment systems. Accordingly, the FSOC Secretariat told us that the designation of retail FMUs is not part of the Council's current work and that it is not possible to estimate when or if retail FMUs will be designated.

FSOC'S Process for Monitoring FMUs

In the preamble to its NPR, the Council proposed, on at least an annual basis, to continue to evaluate whether there are other FMUs that require designation, and whether previous designations of systemically important FMUs should be rescinded. The preamble to the final rule states that the "Council believes that a periodic review of any FMUs that are potentially systemically important, but that have not been designated as such, is important to evaluate any new developments in the roles these FMUs have in the financial system. As a result, the Council anticipates conducting reviews of both designated FMUs and potentially systemically important FMUs on a periodic basis. However, the Council believes that it is important to retain flexibility in the timing for periodic reviews in order to take into account evolving market conditions. Accordingly, the Council is not including a provision regarding periodic reviews in the final rule."

FSOC intends to rely on the designated FMUs' regulators (CFTC, FRB, and SEC) for ongoing reviews. According to the FSOC Secretariat, the regulators provided general updates on the designated FMUs at the December 2012 and March 2013 FMU Committee meetings. The FSOC Secretariat also stated the FMU Committee has discussed the scope and substance of future updates by FMU regulators, such as whether there are any changes in designated FMUs' market share or business plans. At this time, however, there is no agreement or process established in writing that defines the nature, frequency, and communication of such updates.

Furthermore, the FSOC Secretariat stated that the Council is working out a timeline for performing reviews of non-designated FMUs to determine whether any warrant further consideration regarding possible designation. The FSOC Secretariat also stated that this is an ongoing topic of conversation, including at the two most recent quarterly FMU Committee meetings.

While Title VIII does not include specific provisions for the periodic review of both designated and non-designated FMUs, FSOC acknowledged the importance of these activities in its NPR. Further, the preamble to the final rule states that the Council anticipates conducting reviews of both designated FMUs and those that may become systemically important, on a periodic basis. As such, we believe it is important for FSOC to define the nature, frequency, and communication of updates on designated FMUs from the respective FMU regulators and to establish a timeline for periodic reviews of non-designated FMUs that may be systemically important.

Conclusion and Recommendations

We determined that FSOC carried out the activities prescribed in Title VIII by establishing a process and issuing rules to designate FMUs as systemically important, and that it followed the process and rules in designating the FMUs to date. FSOC relied on the work of the FMU Committee during the designation process and voted unanimously to accept the recommendations from the FMU Committee. We did note that the FMU Committee operated without a formal structure and did not keep a record of its meetings. Additionally, FSOC decided not to designate any foreign-based FMUs or PCS activities conducted by financial institutions at this time, although deliberations are on-going. Although the designated FMUs' regulators are conducting on-going monitoring, FSOC has not defined the nature, frequency, and communication of updates on designated FMUs by the FMU regulators, or established a timeline for periodic reviews of non-designated FMUs that may be systemically important.

Accordingly, we recommend that FSOC:

1. Establish a formal structure for the FMU Committee, including designating a chairperson to ensure the proper functioning of the committee, and keeping a record of committee meetings to document, among other things, its deliberations and key recommendations.

   FSOC Response

   FSOC is focused on continuously improving governance over its activities. Council staff is already examining ways to further enhance the governance of the Council's staff committees, and this recommendation will be included as part of that review.

   CIGFO Working Group Comment

   FSOC's commitment to include this recommendation in its current review of ways to enhance the governance of its staff committees is responsive to our recommendation. That said, we believe that establishing a formal structure for the FMU Committee and keeping a record of committee meetings are critical to improved governance.

2. Determine a course of action with regard to foreign-based FMUs consistent with the authorities of Title VIII.

   FSOC Response

   The FMU Committee is expected to continue its discussions on this matter at its upcoming meetings and will communicate any developments to the Deputies Committee and the Council as appropriate.

   CIGFO Working Group Comment

   FSOC's commitment to continue its discussions is responsive to our recommendation. The CIGFO plans to request periodic updates from FSOC on its deliberations and actions regarding foreign-based FMUs.

3. Continue deliberations on the process and rules regarding possible future designation of PCS activities conducted by financial institutions as systemically important.

   FSOC Response

   The FMU Committee is expected to continue its discussions on this matter at its upcoming meetings and will communicate any developments to the Deputies Committee and the Council as appropriate. Proposals for the designation of PCS activities will be considered in the ordinary course of the FMU Committee's work. Specific procedures and rules for the future designation of PCS activities are not being considered by the FMU committee at this time, although such procedures and rules may be developed in the future as a result of FMU Committee discussions or as directed by the Council.

   CIGFO Working Group Comment

   FSOC's commitment to continue its discussions with respect to PCS activities is responsive to our recommendation.

4. Define the nature, frequency, and communication of updates on designated FMUs from the FMU regulators.

   FSOC Response

   The FMU Committee will be asked to continue the work it has begun in this area by proposing specific procedures to address this matter.

   CIGFO Working Group Comment

   FSOC's planned action is responsive to our recommendation. FSOC should establish an estimated timeframe for completing and implementing specific procedures.

5. Establish a timeline for periodic reviews of non-designated FMUs that may be systemically important.

   FSOC Response

   The FMU Committee will be asked to continue the work it has begun in this area by proposing specific procedures to address this matter.

   CIGFO Working Group Comment

   FSOC's planned action is responsive to our recommendation. FSOC should establish an estimated timeframe for completing and implementing specific procedures.

APPENDIX I: Objective, Scope and Methodology

Objective

The audit objective was to assess the application of the rules, procedures, and practices established by FSOC and its members to determine which FMUs should be designated as systemically important and therefore subject to the requirements of Title VIII of the Dodd-Frank Act. This included determining how FSOC established its universe of FMUs and what processes FSOC has going forward to review FMU activity to designate additional FMUs as systemically important and, when appropriate, to rescind an FMU designation.

Scope and Methodology

The scope of this audit included the process FSOC used to designate eight FMUs as systemically important in July 2012 and its processes going forward to review FMU activity.

To accomplish our objective, we:

- interviewed representatives of FSOC's member agencies through the use of a structured questionnaire. We designed the questionnaire to determine and review FSOC's process for designating FMUs as systemically important, and to solicit information on the FSOC member agencies' involvement in the process as well as their views on how the process worked. We developed the questions based on designation process activities outlined in Title VIII of the Dodd-Frank Act. We also obtained relevant documentation from the FSOC member agencies;

- reviewed the ANPR, NPR, the final rule, and an overview of the planned FMU designation process for the purpose of determining conformity with Title VIII;

- compared information on FMUs obtained from FSOC with information we obtained from FSOC member agencies that regulate FMUs; and

- reviewed other related documentation such as FMU Committee membership information, FMU metrics data, recommendation memorandums on FMUs prepared for the Council, FMU notification letters, and FMU Committee meeting invitations and agendas. As noted in our report, the FMU Committee did not keep a record of its meetings, so we obtained testimonial evidence about its proceedings.

We performed audit fieldwork from February through April 2013. We conducted this performance audit in accordance with generally accepted government auditing standards. Those standards require that we plan and perform the audit to obtain sufficient, appropriate evidence to provide a reasonable basis for our findings and conclusions based on our audit objective. We believe that the evidence obtained provides a reasonable basis for our findings and conclusions based on our audit objective.

APPENDIX II:
Timeline of Significant FMU Designation Events

Date	Event
12/21/2010	FSOC published an advance notice of proposed rulemaking regarding the designation criteria in section 804 of Title VIII. (75 Fed. Reg. 79,982)
3/28/2011	FSOC published a notice of proposed rulemaking regarding the designation criteria in section 804 of Title VIII. (76 Fed. Reg. 17,047)
7/27/2011	FSOC published its final rule outlining the criteria, processes, and procedures for the designation of FMUs. (76 Fed. Reg. 44,763) The final rule notes that FSOC expects to address the designation of payment, clearing, or settlement activities as systemically important in a separate rulemaking.
12/19/2011	The FMU Committee sent a memo through the Deputies Committee to the Council recommending that eight FMUs move from Stage One to Stage Two of the designation process.
12/21/2011	FSOC voted unanimously to advance the eight FMUs from Stage One to Stage Two of the designation process.
1/4/2012	FSOC sent written notification to the eight FMUs of the Council's consideration for designation of their company as systemically important. The notification letters also invited the FMUs to submit information about their companies to FSOC by February 3, 2012.
5/10/2012	Members of the FMU Committee met with the Clearing House Payments Company L.L.C., at the company's request. The meeting focused on the company's concerns regarding the competitive implications of being designated.
5/22/2012	FSOC unanimously approved the proposed designation of the eight FMUs as systemically important. FSOC sent written notification to the designated FMUs. The notification letters also informed the FMUs that they had 30 days to request a hearing if they disagreed with the proposed determination of the Council or the Council's proposed findings of fact. None of the designated FMUs requested such a hearing.
7/18/2012	After voting unanimously on May 22, 2012, to designate the eight FMUs as systemically important, FSOC sent written notification to the eight FMUs.

APPENDIX III:
Description of Designated FMUs

Company	Description
The Clearing House Payments Company, L.L.C., on the basis of its role as operator of the Clearing House Interbank Payments System (CHIPS)	The Clearing House Payments Company, L.L.C. is the world's largest private sector payments operator and the legal entity that operates CHIPS, which is a multilateral system operated for the purposed of transferring payments among its 52 participants. The 52 participants are U.S. commercial banks, foreign banks with offices in the U.S., and one private banker. These participants constitute some of the largest banks in the world by asset size and include bank subsidiaries of 22 financial institutions considered to be global systemically important financial institutions by the Financial Stability Board.[15] An important feature of CHIPS is that it can bilaterally and multilaterally net payments for settlement. CHIPS is the only private sector system in the U.S. for settling large-value U.S. dollar payments continuously throughout the day. CHIPS settles approximately $1.6 trillion on average per day.
CLS Bank International	CLS Bank International operates the largest multicurrency cash settlement system to mitigate settlement risk for the foreign exchange transactions of its members, who are financial institutions, and their customers. Through its services, CLS Bank International significantly reduces settlement risk and provides substantial liquidity savings through its use of multilateral net funding. CLS Bank International settles an average daily value of 4.77 trillion U.S. dollar equivalent, representing 68 percent of foreign exchange market activity in CLS Bank-eligible currencies and products.
Chicago Mercantile Exchange, Inc.	Chicago Mercantile Exchange, Inc. (CME) is one of the largest central counterparty clearing services providers in the world, clearing 96 percent of the entire market for U.S. futures, options on futures, and commodity options. CME provides central counterparty clearing services for futures, options, and swaps that can be used by market participants for a variety of purposes. In 2011, CME cleared contracts with an average daily gross notional value in the trillions of U.S. dollars and average daily gross notional values in the millions of U.S. dollars of over-the-counter credit default swaps.
The Depository Trust Company	The Depository Trust Company (DTC) serves as the central securities depository for substantially all corporate and municipal debt and equity securities available for trading in the U.S. DTC is a wholly owned subsidiary of the Depository Trust & Clearing Corporation. DTC provides securities movements for National Securities Clearing Corporation's net settlements, and settlement for institutional trades (which typically involve money and securities transfers between custodian banks and broker/dealers), as well as money market instruments. In 2011, DTC maintained custody and ownership records for approximately $39.5 trillion in securities. The peak daily gross value of transactions processed by DTC in 2011 was equal to $728.8 billion.

---

15 The Financial Stability Board was established to coordinate at the international level the work of national financial authorities and international standard setting bodies and to develop and promote the implementation of effective regulatory, supervisory and other financial sector policies. Its members include national authorities responsible for financial stability, international financial institutions, sector-specific international groups of regulators and supervisors, and committees of central bank experts. The U.S. members on the board are FRB, SEC, and Treasury.

Company	Description
Fixed Income Clearing Corporation	Fixed Income Clearing Corporation (FICC) plays a prominent role in the fixed income market as the sole clearing agency in the U.S. acting as a central counterparty and provider of significant clearance and settlement services for cash-settled U.S. Treasury and agency securities and the non-private mortgage-backed securities markets. FICC is a wholly owned subsidiary of the Depository Trust & Clearing Corporation. FICC is made up of two divisions, the Government Securities Division (FICC/GSD) and the Mortgage Backed Securities Division (FICC/MBSD), each providing clearing services in a different portion of the fixed income market. In 2011, FICC/GSD processed 40.5 million transactions in U.S. government and agency securities worth $1.1 quadrillion on a gross basis. Through multilateral netting, FICC/GSD reduced the value of financial obligations requiring settlement in 2011 from $1.1 quadrillion to $230 trillion. In 2011, FICC/MBSD processed mortgage backed securities transactions worth approximately $64.8 trillion, which through multilateral netting was reduced in value to $3 trillion.
ICE Clear Credit LLC	ICE Clear Credit LLC (ICE Clear Credit) is the world's largest clearinghouse for credit default swaps. ICE Clear Credit clears a majority of the credit default swap products in the U.S. that are eligible for clearing by a central counterparty. ICE Clear Credit is the only clearinghouse worldwide that clears foreign sovereign credit default swaps. Since 2009, ICE Clear Credit has cleared over 300,000 credit default swap transactions whose notional value is in the trillions of U.S. dollars. In 2011, ICE Clear Credit cleared a peak daily gross volume of 7,222 index contracts, 14,708 single-name contracts, and 5,680 sovereign contracts.
National Securities Clearing Corporation	National Securities Clearing Corporation (NSCC) provides clearing, settlement, risk management, central counterparty services and a guarantee of completion for certain transactions for virtually all broker-to-broker trades involving equities, corporate and municipal debt, American depository receipts, exchange-traded funds, and unit investment trusts. NSCC is a wholly owned subsidiary of Depository Trust and Clearing Corporation. In 2011, the corporation cleared $220.7 trillion worth of trades on a gross basis, which represented nearly all broker-to-broker equity and debt trades executed on the major U.S. exchanges and most other equity trading venues.
The Options Clearing Corporation	The Options Clearing Corporation is the world's largest equity derivatives clearing organization. The types of options cleared include those on equities, indices, currency, and commodities though equity options accounted for approximately 93 percent of total clearing volume. The corporation is the sole issuer and settling agent for all stock options, equity index options, and single-stock futures listed on U.S. exchanges. The dollar value and volume of options transactions handled by the Options Clearing Corporation includes substantially all of the equity options traded on U.S. options exchanges. The peak daily gross volume for the corporation in 2011 was approximately 41.5 million option contracts, 383,000 futures contracts, and 89.3 million stock loan shares.

Source: FSOC 2012 Annual Report and websites of the FMUs

APPENDIX IV: FSOC Response

DEPARTMENT OF THE TREASURY
WASHINGTON, D.C.

UNDER SECRETARY

June 17, 2013

The Honorable Eric M. Thorson
Chair, Council of Inspectors General
on Financial Oversight (CIGFO)
1500 Pennsylvania Avenue, NW
Washington, D.C. 20220

Re: Response to CIGFO's Draft Audit Report: *Audit of the Financial Stability Oversight Council's Designation of Financial Market Utilities: Report to the Financial Stability Oversight Council and the Congress*

Dear Mr. Chairman:

Thank you for the opportunity to review and respond to your draft Audit Report, *Audit of the Financial Stability Oversight Council's Designation of Financial Market Utilities: Report to the Financial Stability Oversight Council and the Congress*, dated June 2013 (the Report). The Financial Stability Oversight Council (Council) and its members and member agencies appreciate the Council of Inspectors General on Financial Oversight (CIGFO) Working Group's review of the processes and procedures used by the Council to designate eight financial market utilities (FMUs) as systemically important. This letter responds, on behalf of the Secretary of the Treasury as Chairperson of the Council, to the Report. The staffs of Council members and member agencies previously provided comments and technical suggestions to CIGFO staff.

The Dodd-Frank Wall Street Reform and Consumer Protection Act (Dodd-Frank Act) authorizes the Council to designate an FMU as "systemically important" if the Council determines that the failure of or a disruption to the functioning of the FMU could create, or increase, the risk of significant liquidity or credit problems spreading among financial institutions or markets and thereby threaten the stability of the U.S. financial system. Designated FMUs become subject to the heightened prudential and supervisory provisions of Title VIII of the Dodd-Frank Act.

CIGFO found that the Council carried out the designation activities as established in the Dodd-Frank Act. CIGFO also found that the Designations of FMUs and Payment, Clearing, and Settlement Activities Committee (FMU Committee) carried out its activities in the designation process as intended by the Council. CIGFO further concluded that the Council carried out the activities prescribed in the Dodd-Frank Act by establishing a process and issuing rules to designate FMUs as systemically important, and that the Council followed that process and those rules in designating the eight FMUs in 2012.

In addition to these findings, CIGFO makes five recommendations to the Council. First, CIGFO recommends that the Council establish a formal structure for the FMU Committee, including designating a chairperson and keeping a record of meetings to document, among other things, its key recommendations. Although the FMU Committee documented all of its recommendations to the Council, the Council nevertheless is focused on continuously improving governance over its activities. Council staff is already examining ways to further enhance the governance of the Council's staff committees, and this recommendation will be included as part of that review.

The next two recommendations are that the Council should continue its deliberations on the process and rules regarding the possible future designation of payment, clearing, or settlement (PCS) activities carried out by one or more financial institutions as systemically important; and that the Council should determine a course of action with regard to foreign-based FMUs consistent with the authorities of Title VIII. As noted in the Report, the FMU Committee is expected to continue its discussion of both of these matters at its upcoming meetings. Consistent with its practice thus far, the FMU Committee would communicate any developments to the Deputies Committee and the Council as appropriate. Proposals for the designation of PCS activities or additional FMUs will be considered in the ordinary course of the FMU Committee's work based on the facts and circumstances of the individual proposal. Specific procedures and rules for the future designation of PCS activities are not being considered by the FMU Committee at this time, although such procedures and rules may be developed in the future as a result of FMU Committee discussions or as directed by the Council.

The final two recommendations are that the Council should define the nature, frequency, and communication of updates on designated FMUs from the FMU regulators; and that the Council should establish a timeline for periodic reviews of non-designated FMUs that may be systemically important. As Chairperson of the Council's Deputies Committee, I will ask the FMU Committee to continue the work it has begun in these areas by proposing specific procedures to address both of these matters.

Thank you again for the opportunity to review and comment on the Report. We recognize that CIGFO has an important oversight role, and we value CIGFO's input and recommendations. The Council looks forward to working with you in the future.

Sincerely,

Mary J. Miller

APPENDIX V: CIGFO Working Group

Department of the Treasury – Lead Agency

Eric M. Thorson, Inspector General, Department of the Treasury, and CIGFO Chair

Theresa Cameron	Marla Freedman	Clyburn Perry III
Jeff Dye	Michael Maloney	Bob Taylor
April Ellison	Susan Marshall	

Board of Governors of the Federal Reserve System

Jason Derr	Eva Su
Anna Saez	Michael VanHuysen

Commodity Futures Trading Commission

Tony Baptiste

Federal Deposit Insurance Corporation

Travis Sumner	Peggy Wolf

Federal Housing Finance Agency

Katie Kimmel	Tara Lewis	Andrew W. Smith

National Credit Union Administration

Marvin Stith

Securities and Exchange Commission

Kelli Brown-Barnes	Steve Kaffen	William Garay
Jacqueline Wilson		

Special Inspector General for the Troubled Asset Relief Program

Jessica Byars	Jonathan Lebruto